Modern Amazigh Poetry: Selected Poems

Mohammed Ouagrar
Translated by
Mustapha Akhoullou

Contents

Preface 1

The Poems in English 11

The Smile (Azmumg) 11

The Mirror (Tisit) 12

Earth, O Earth! (Akal, a akal!) 14

The Curse (Tagat) 15

I am too busy (Ur iyyid yagh) 16

Unique (WaZ) 17

The Vagabond (AhyyaD) 19

Amazigh 20

Alienation (Azwag) 20

Rabies (IsiD) 21

Dizziness (Timlillay) 21

The Witness (Inigi n duf) 22

Hold on! (Sagwmamt ak!) 25

The Truth and The Illusion (IbiDi d Tidit) 28

The Poems in Amazigh 31

Azmumg (The Smile) 31

Tisit (The Mirror) 32

Akal, a akal! (Earth, O Earth!)................ 34

Tagat (The Curse) 35

Ur iyyid yagh (I Am Too Busy) 36

WaZ! (Unique!).. 37

AhyyaD (The Vagabond) 38

Amazigh.. 39

Azwag (Alienation) 40

iSiD (Rabies).. 41

Timlillay (Dizziness) 42

Inigi n Duf (The Witness) 42

Saggwmamt akw! (Hold On!)............ 46

IbiDi d Tidit (The Truth and The Illusion)... 51

Preface

As you read this preface, I hope you recognize that I am here only an empirical reader of such a highly distinguished Amazigh poet whose poetic texts are always in search of implied readers whose role is to read beyond the literal meaning of the words so as to grasp their "poetic and stylistic significance". But this is not to say that these texts imply "ideal" readers, for such a claim would be detrimental to the humanistic and artistic value of the artwork itself. And here we need to ask a simple question : Is not the translator himself this implied reader? Hereafter, this prefatory statement has been put agonistically and hesitantly because the subject itself demands enough intellectual aptitude and competence in order to yield itself into some economical phraseology.

In the Ouagrar's poems translated by Mustapha Akhoullou, we see that unity of a man with the universe that is sought after outside ideological forms or moral imperatives. Poetry, after all, is a return to the self. Such a unity seemed to be attained in certain epiphanic moments in Ouagrar's poetry, for it is itself an experience of the soul, of the freeing of the self; "Be who you want / And be who you are/ But find yourself". It is this quest for the self that I find illuminating in Ouagrar's poetry which is profoundly immersed in the rhythms of Nature.

It seems to me that the most challenging problematic in translating Ouagrar's poetry relates to his prolific use of the poetic image, metaphoricity and literary wording. Roughly speaking, it is never easy to pinpoint the aesthetic and literary affiliations of Ouagrar's poetry; some would say Ouagrar is a modernist *avant la lettre* but I would go further and claim that there is more to Ouagrar's Oeuvre than its modernist tendency. I think that the difficulty in assessing Ouagrar's poems at hand has less to do with its relationship with modernism than with the sort of poetry we encounter in his Oeuvre which is highly tainted and immersed in Amazigh culture and tradition. It should be noted here that the profuse cultural legacy of Amazigh tradition embodied in orality weighs heavily on the poetry of Mohammed Ouagrar. To fall short of the competence to read into the deepest cultural and symbolic meanings which are deeply imbedded in Ouagrar's peotry is to fall below the demands of an implied reader whose role is to read between and beyond the poetic lines. In this context, it is rewarding to apprehend that translation is a cultural phenomenon before it is anything else, but the cultural is already imbedded in the poetic and hence in need of excavation from the part of an adequate translator. It must be highlighted here that the role of the translator is not just to communicate or transmit the manifest and the hidden meanings of the original work, but also to elongate the life of the poem in its target language.

In Ouagrar's poem "The Smile", for instance, we notice a simultaneity of the image, for we can see that the poem forgounds a dialectic image of the sacred and the profane. There are here two types of diction which are being juxtaposed in the poem. The first type belongs to the physical realm of experience (smile, lust, lips, lipstik) as paralleled with a symbolically metaphisical lexus (flood, limbo, the sun, ashes, wind).

The dialectic image is always characterized by the synchroneity of its images. Thereafter, in "The Smile", the simultaneous images are both life and death, lust and apathy, beauty and hideousness. But this is not to say that the construction of the image here is oppositional. Rather, it is an organic dialectic which qualitatively and continuously leads into the open, into "Light" which is dampened by darkness; The Smile vanished/ In your lips. Again the image of the Sun is important in the Amazigh culture, for it opens a counter-discursive anthropological space which highlights the importance of the popular in Ouagrar's poetry. It is not the space here to extensively comment on this issue, but the image of the Sun, as an example, should not be read only in terms of its metaphorical meaning, but also in relation to its symbolic and allegorical meanings in the Amazigh culture. The process of appreciating this poetry would be inconceivable in the absence of this aesthetic model of cultural symbolism which lies deeply rooted in the Amazigh culture and language and any translation which does not take this cultural dimension into account is likely to misconstrue the meanings of the original text.

I really do believe that Ouagrar's poems as translated in this highly rewarding book found its chosen translator in Mustapha

Akhoullou who painstakingly worked on these poems not only with the eye of an adequate translator, but also with the passionate interest of someone who has been scrupulously remained an attentive reader and critic of Amazigh poetry with the requisite competence and alacrity to treat this poetry properly. For me, Akhoullou's translation of Ouagrar is my first encounter with a text translated from the Amazigh language into English and in the experience of reading it, I see this translation as a serious attempt to come to terms with the forgeinness imbedded in the source and target languages. But I need also to stress out here that no matter how a translation is good, it will never represent the significance of the original text. For any translation from one language to another entails a shift in meaning and a both linguistic and cultural disparity between the original text and the translation. What is interesting in Ouagrar's poems and Akhoullou's translation is the effect of the dialectical movement that keeps us always shifting between the two in order to unravel the meanings behind the words.

As the scope of the preface does not allow for detours, I should reiterate here that the symbolic and the cultural dimensions of Ouagrar's Oeuvre merit our attention, and that Mustapha Akhollou — with the eye of an implied reader and translator — has provided us with an excellent rendition of these dimensions throughout this translation; a translation which has helped me to roughly sharpen my understanding of Ouagrar's poems in this book. Thus a special acknowledgment and recognition must go to this deeply valued friend who has proved his reputation both as a fierce reader of Amazigh poetry and as a conscientious translator. I am grateful to him first for sending me the first and the last drafts of this book and, second, for kindly allowing me to write this preface on his behalf.

Rachid Ait Abdelmouman

The Poems in English

The Smile (Azmumg)

The smile stretched
Lust begotten.
I strove to swim
But drowned.
The smile vanished
In your lips.
Then I was buried away
By the flood,
And tossed in the limbo.
Yet, The Sun brought me back to life.

Now I beseech you
Take me,
Crush me,
Make me ashes,
Sift me,
Convert me to lipstick,
For your lips.

If not,
Blow me in the wind.
I shall never come back
To fight
Inside the nest
That gave birth
To your smile.

The Mirror (Tisit)

O myself!

I am missing you!

I look at you in the mirror.
I stand still.
You praise and you satirize.
Sometimes you laugh, and

Sometimes you weep.
Sometimes you smile, and
Sometimes you yell.
Sometimes you frown, and
Sometimes you whistle.

I am the serpent,
And you are my shredded skin.
I am your nest,
And you are my track.

You are the rainbow,
And you are the hail.
I am the tears of high summer.
I tried to embrace you,
But you poked me in the eye.

You punched me with you hand,
And the mirror shattered to pieces,
And you vanished

In me.
When I wanted to grab a piece,
You wounded me,
And left a scar.
Longing came back to haunt me.
O my aloof self!
I'm missing you!

Earth, O Earth! (Akal, a akal!)

"Moon, O moon!
Please, hold the sky!"
We are not even sure
Whether Above goes with the moon,
Or we fear that one day
The sky would fall over the earth!
When the Late Armstrong stepped on the moon,
He saw the earth
Just like the Moon
Shining above.
"Earth, O earth!
Please, hold the sky!"

The Curse (Tagat)

I have not, I am not.
I would never have existed
If life hadn't said to the curse:
"Ma'am,
Have your home here."
I am the heir of a limited supply,
I have the feet of the vagabond.
Always on the move.
They resist settlement.
They chase the mirage
In their horizon.
I have not, I am not.
I would never have
Borne false witness
Against this life.

I am too busy (Ur iyyid yagh)

The rivers of poems are up there.
The oceans of music are up here.
My beloved is the boat.
My paddles are rebab[1] and lutar.[2]
I am hunting.
Amidst the waves of wine
And others of darkness,
I am patiently seeking light
In the eyes of my beloved.
I bid farewell to myself
In her eyes.
And we embraced.
O myself!
I am too busy
To come back!

---

[1] Rebab is a one-stringed, bowed instrument strictly used by the Amazigh musicians in the south of Morocco.

[2] Lutar is a plucked lute unique to Berber music in Morocco. It has three strings, and is found mostly in the Middle Atlas region.

Unique (WaZ)

What a lovely day
Your day is!
How unique she is
Among the other days!
Who trimmed the fringe of her
morning
Above her eyes?
Who tinted the scarlet lips
On her mouth?
Who adjusted the beaded
necklace
Around her neck?
Her chest is immuned
With the golden wheat.
Her noon's waist is belted
With the rays of the sun.
Her afternoon is the brook.
The blooming plants
Are covering the hills.
The sun lines the eyes
Of her twilight
Before she goes down.

The moon rises
And announces the night
To attend asays.[3]
Dating all night long,
Ululations,
Songs,
And poems.
What a lovely day
Your day is!
How unique she is
Among the other days!

---

[3] Asays is a very ancient outdoor circular theater in North Africa used by the Amazigh people for different purposes including tribal celebrations and meetings

The Vagabond (AhyyaD)

I am the flying ant
I am the bush
I am the beehive dowser
I am the stones of the river
I am the steam of the soup
I am the seeds of the ray
I am the passerby
I am done
I am the foam of the frankincense
I am the vagabond
Who picks up things
And forgets the bag
Forgets the tool
Satisfied with alms
And sinks in the abyss
Tempted by longing
I am the be
In the loop.

Amazigh

I am the farm plot
I am the salted soil
I am the rust of the steel
I salt the unsalted
My heart is the entrance.
Yet, not accessible to anything
Brought by the stream.

Alienation (Azwag)

Be prepared for alienation
O you who seek the Truth!
Be the vagabond
And go.
You will learn
Till you know
That you don't know.
You will be seeking
The head of the thread
Until you're lost,
You will befriend insomnia,
You will be the companion
Of the curse,

And you will endure in silence.

Rabies (IsiD)

That rabid convention
Reigns with an iron fist.
It pisses me off.
Who lifted you
And forgot the smash?
I will lift you to the extreme
And smash you
On the ground.

Dizziness (Timlillay)

It would surely be good
If one tilts,
And complains
About dizziness
Through dizziness
To dizziness.
I miss dizziness,
O dizziness!

The Witness (Inigi n duf)

Oh wave!
I saw the reflection of the moon
Scattered on you.
Is it caressing you?
Is it licking you?
Or
Leading you?
Oh wave!
Hasty that you are!
You are already on your
destination.
Where are you running?
You brought up all the talk,
All the criticism,
Just tell me
Noble wave
Where are you running?
Omni-sea man I am,
And I know
For you,
Your witness I am,
Lucky you!

Yet, tell me where,
Where are you running?
I think it's better for you
To roll back,
Can't you?
Instead of riding your rage!
Where to?
Too much noise,
Too much turbid,
Too much madness,
You trust your wandering feet
And you don't even know
Where they are taking you!
Your insomnia is tamed.
Tell me where,
Where are you running?
High as you are!
Your height is thick!
I am wondering,
What is that you're chasing!
Where are you running?
You found the rod
Lurking with a hook
Before your height.
When it bows,

It is only grazing its share
In your journey.
You went by unnoticed,
Vanished in the shore,
Became foam,
Or clashed in the rocks.
The rod stood still.
You see,
Stubborn is your height,
Your witness is only right
In the time yet to come.
Just tell me, wave,
Where are you rushing?
Where to?

Hold on! (Sagwmamt ak!)

Magnetized I am
By the necklace
In her cleavage.
Sacred is the Now!
Besieged by the divine Henna in your palms,
From where I sipped the wine-drop.
Is it true?
Did you grab it
From the steam
Leaked out
From your mirror?
Be it as it may,
Here it is now flowing.
Hold on!
You are as expected!
My sip please,
Be my guest
And I will be yours
I will have you in my mouth.
My mouth, Hold on!

Wait until I speak,
Until I dot the i's and cross the t's:
A happy man I am.
My soup is only a single bean.
To sew,
I borrow the needle.
My Season will find me
Patiently waiting.
Then the Now and the Here
Shall utterly be mine.
Hold on!
You rode the waves of lust
Its ocean tossed you on my shore,
Splosh!
Hold on!
You tried to let go
Your paddle,
And you weren't attentive.
Then you sank in you.
Maybe I need to eat
To be able to host you.
The drunk soul
Made you thirsty.
You journeyed across the throat.
You wanted to sneeze

But you shouted!
And you quarreled with the
tongue.
Then
Throat pain dizziness emerged.
That's too much.
You wet,
You sweat,
Nausea,
You're aching,
Hey!
Hold on!

The Truth and The Illusion (IbiDi d Tidit)

Born and bloomed
Between the have-never and the will-never
I can't be erased.
Ago, in it,
 Nothing happened.
The same with you tomorrow.
In you,
Nothing shall happen.

Give yourself a break.
Above all,
Drop your arms,
Await your Now.
Let go your bygones,
Forget,
And get rid of the mud
Left inside.

Time travels on.
I don't care!

Bid it farewell
Bury your past
And forget it.
Never await time-to-come.
The now-here is your essence.
You are the share in-between

O my dear!
You are the core.
Live it
Sink in it
Be it.

Tell me O darkness!
Where do you go
When I switch on the light?
Shadows are but illusions,
Ask the Sun

So as to know.
Relax!

Be who you want,

And be who you are.

But find yourself.

Adhere to this virtue.
For, your departure is imminent.
Don't let the noise of thinking
Vex your conscience.
Vacuum the link.
Be prepared for your tomb
Until the soul leaves you
To join the source,
Our mother,
Light.

The Poems in Amazigh

Azmumg (The Smile)

Immizzeg uzmumg.
Izuzzer amarg
Uremgh ad chefegh
Gedegh.
S igh iddem uzmumg
I tinfurin.
Izri ungi
Yasi d assar,
Ig iyyi bayttar.
Ifel iyi gigh tassika.
Izenzaren ar agh zerrun.
Ttergh gim, a mar!
Asi iyi
Temzit iyi
Tessift iyi
Teg t iyi d uzwigh
I tinfurin

Negh iyi tgit d waDu.
Ad nn issendu.
Gh useddi lli gh ilul,
Uzmumg nnunt.

Tisit (The Mirror)

Ikhf inu
Yagh iyi umarg nnun
Aggwgh nn s is gh tisit
Nkk siyyagh
Ur ar ttmussugh
Ar iyi ittalgh
Ar iyi isignit
Yat gh a- yalla
Yat gh a-ittṣṣa
Yat gh isskernser ignzi
Yat gh izmumg i taḍṣa
Yat gh a-ittwagh
Yat gh a-isnSig
Dars agharas
Dari tansa
Nttan asray
Nkkin ablinka
Dars tislit n unẓaṛ

D briru
Dari imṭṭawn n ijiwi
Gigh nn ad t ssudngh
Ikkeḍ iyi
Ig d afus ad iyi yut
Tg tisit izlallayn
Iddm iyi
Gigh nn ad grugh azlallay
Ibḍel iyi
Ifl d azmul
Yaḍu d umarg
Ils iyi
Ikhf inu, nkk d itun
Ku yan
Ma gh t iga uḍaṛ ns
Ikhf inu
Ingha iyi umarg nnun.

Akal, a akal! (Earth, O Earth!)

"ayyur, a ayyuri!
i rbbi ayt a ayyur
amZ ukan
ignwani!"
ur sss
is yad nghal
is nn illa nig gh wayyur
ngh d
is nit nksuD
ad iDr ignna f wakal
ass ann gh nn iga igllin n Armstrong
aDar gh wayyur yanni d akak iZil
s ufulki iga zund ayyur
akal, a akal!
i rbbi ayt a akal
amZ ukan
ignwani!

Tagat (The Curse)

ur dari, ur gigh.

ur akkw imil,

rad iligh.

is ka tenna

tudert i tagat:

ham, am ma tigemmi nem.

ssiligh awelk

da d ufigh

yiri iyi uDar

ad afudegh

icha aZellug

f ad myaren.

imdi nn marur

gh idir nes.

ur dari, ur gigh.

ur akkw imil,

rad asigh

tugga n uzenbu
f tudert ad.

Ur iyyid yagh (I Am Too Busy)

Hann isaffen n turar
Had ilalen n uzawan
Ig winu agherrabu
Tukkla rribab d lutar
Nekkin ar gwemmergh.
Taddangiwin n unZir
Tiyyad n tillas.
Tamegh nn tifawt
Gh wallen n winu
Gawergh.
Ttelgh as
Ittel iyi d afus,
Rraghutegh ikhf inu
Gh iZri nnun.
Ur iyi d sik yagh
A ikhf nu
Ad ak d urrigh.

WaZ! (Unique!)

Mk ad ifulki wass ad nem
iga waZ ngr ussan!
mad as imgrn i taylgi ns
tawnza gh gr wallen
mad as ighwman gh imi ns
uzwigh i tinfurin
mad as yuglen gh tmggredt
aqqayn n uzellay ?
tadmert, nttat,
irden n uregh igzi tnt
tbikks as tiddi i imrZi ns
s uznezer n tafurkt
takkwZin targwa n waman
tfsu nn tuga gh wafatn
tiwwutchi ns tZul as tafukt
fadd ann ghawlent
ighwli d wayyur ibrreh i tiyyids
nili nn gh usays
ig iD nnunt asqar s kigan
taghwrit,astara d tizlatin
mk ad ifulki wass ad nem

awzeghi is ila anaw ngr ussan!

Mk ad ifulki wass ad nem
iga waZ ngr ussan!

AhyyaD (The Vagabond)

Gigh uttif
Gigh agwntif
D maf agwlif
Gigh irigw n uzkkif
Gigh tiwwuna
Gigh kra izgren tabrida
Gigh irden n tiffilla
Gigh ma nn izrin!
Gigh ahiyyaD ann
D islayn tighawsiwin
Ittu tawlekt,ittu imiss
Yawi nn timillut
Iddem i war
Igli t umarg
Imal d mk ann.

Amazigh

gigh uzun.
Gigh amersal.
tanikt i wuzzal.
yan ur ilin taDfi,
gegh asen tt.
ig ul inu,
taginant.
ur d wanna d ukan,
igli usaru,
rZemgh as.

Azwag (Alienation)

yan isiggilen

Titt n tidit

ad ibiks I uzwag

ig ahiyyaD, iterm.

ad tent d akkw ikk;

ar d d ur ikk

awd yat gisent.

rad iDfer gh ifili

ikhf ar d itelf,

iggammi ad as tent d

ikk iDs, iwzent as.

ig asmun i tagat,

ar tent ittagwem, ifiss.

iSiD (Rabies)

atig an gh illa iSiD
ibaD
s ighil n uzzal
ur as nnigh a mar!
ma ak yullen
ar ghilli gh a d tturrit
ittu k in?!
nekki ra ak allegh
ar ghilli gh a d ur tturrit
utegh sik akal.

Timlillay (Dizziness)

Ifulki nit
Y an ismammin
F timlillay
S timlillay
I timlillay
Yan ikkan,
I genna
Ur ikka
Akal.
Yagh iyi umarg
A timlillay.

Inigi n Duf (The Witness)

Ẓrigh g im
idumsal n wayyur
A lalla taḍḍinga
Izd is ar km ttḥlliln
Izd is akm ttllghn
negh dd is km glin ?!

Mani s di tusit assar
A lalla taḍḍinga
Yam man tigira

Ra nn tkhsit gh taghart
Mani ttghawalt ?!

Mad am d ikwman
A taḍḍinga
ghadd n uzawar
ghadd n tdwwayt
Mlamt iyi a-ma
Mani ttghawalt ?!

Nkkin gigh angwmar
khaldgh awnt
Ammuttl d wanan
iligh iyyt gh iggi
Ddaw am
Nigh mnid nnunt
Nkkin gigh inigi nnunt
irghud awnt
Mani ttghawalt ?!

A s nnigh yuf...
Yuf awnt ukan
Mr add is tsmunemt
Twerrimt ḍaṛat
Mach tggummimt
Ad tsghalmt tugga inu
Ayhayya nnunt

Tssudumt iṣiḍ nnunt
Mani ttghawaalt ?!

Midd n tazat
Midd n iṛiẓ
Midd n unufl
Ur yad tssenmt
Mani s kwnt
igli uḍar
igrd iwiz nnunt
Afud izug awnt
ayuz nnunt !
Mani ttghawalt ?!

Tattuyt a taḍḍinga
Tsdusmt nit i tiddi nnunt
Mlamt iyi ka
Righ ad issangh
Ma f ar tẓẓdmt
iẓnirn nnunt
Man arwass ann
LLi ttghwmmact
Mani ttghawalt ?!

Tuffit di taghanimt
issmdi d ifssi nns aṣnsi
i tiddi nnunt

igh yad awnt kwnant
is nn ka ksant
i taghamt nns
gh ummuddu nnunt
Wayyahu nnunt
Mani ttghawalt ?!

Tzrit a taḍḍinga
Zunn ur tzrit !
Taghwd tiddi lli n tghanimt
Tsllaw nn gh umlal
Tg aluss
Negh nn tfruri gh ujaṛif
Tach ultt tach
Lli igan tiddi nnunt
Ur ar ittighwẓin ar imal
inigi nnunt !
Akhayt,wayyahu nnunt
Mani ttghawalt ?

Saggwmamt akw! (Hold On!)

Izzug iyi nn
uZllay d idran
Gh tadmrt ns
D Agwrram
Kud ad
Gh didi tllamt
Wa mkad am t ghwmant
Kud gh iyi mmallint
Ghad n tdlkin
Sugh gisnt
Nit
Is tt id tgwrit
Gh tZirrit
Turddem
D iriggw mu nn
Tssmdit tisit?

Iqd iyt iriggw
Ngh ulban
Hat id ghil ghil
TssiwD angi
Gisn tmqqit
Saggwmamt akkw
Mk da gim
Ira uzmz
Ka nn gitunt ntam
Sakamt a tugwmimt iw
imikk imi nnunt
Sakgh kwnt nkkin
i kigan d imi nw
saggwmamt akkw
saggwmat a imi nu
ar d nsawal
ar d zwar nissan
mani s tiwimt
a tayyuga imassn

zzig-gh azkkif
gh ibiw iw
tassmi n urttal
a taba nw a lall
ka s ar gnnugh
ffig bdda aman
f usga
saqsamt g igi
hmmus
bu usaragn
ur akkw ar nkk
tnt ttjaragh
ar d ukan d lkmnt
ilmma
kud ad dari ghi
da sdukkunt isan
saggwmamt akkw
tssudamt d siti
tayyught n taDfi

igr d situnt
gh taghart iw
ill ns
izbu kwnt inn itts
tghawlmt
tgDmt nn gitunt
mmiqq
nighlamt akkw
zzigh d
turmemt nn tibDit
d taglut nm
is nn akkw
fllas tbbimt
adwal nm
yam ur d is iyi d
gitunt tgwmr tizi n tirmt
zund kra
s hra d ka
suddmn isalasn

angha agh d isskwna

iman illugman

irifi nnunt

tffrtl amt tnzi

tzzigt taghuyit

tilimt nn d ils

gh umsiriD

ittlamt uzghagh

d ugurzu n ugrD

tazgganzart

tkka nn darunt

tawnamt tajjayt

d trghi n taqqayt

wa tchiDmt nn

khwDi ur iyi akkw

kwnt inn tunfmt

tibdigt

tzazzrt s tidi

tatst nn tammumDi

ibdr km unusm

yisli km lhal

tgguntimt nn zikk

gh tmlillay

qq

saggwmamt akkw.

IbiDi d Tidit (The Truth and The Illusion)

gr jju d sar

agh d nlula

mmghigh

ur ufigh ad akufgh

gam gis

ur jjun ijRi yat

mkann d imal

a imal

ur sar gik ijRi yat

sunfu ak

slawan d akkw ak

aqryan gr sis

saggwm s kud ann

d sgudi n kud lli

ssiki tn

rraghut ak tn

iriZ ka nn ssrghan

gh ugnsu nk

tizi nttat tssuda

nkk

ma mu tt za righ

msifiD dis

mDl ak nn

gam nk

tettut t

ad ak ur ttql

s imal ann

d itrmn

ghil d ghid nnun

yas nutni
ad k igan
mmldan k a winu
mmallin k
ddr ak tn
s tiddi
tighzi
d turrut
udan k
gD ak nn gisn
dr awn
i isdram nsn
mani tkkamt
a tillas
igh ddigh ar d amt ssRghagh
asid
saqsa ak
tafukt da igan tafukt
imula ur gin amr ibiDi

frk ak asn

ka

sar nk

ad ur tettut

ad tsiyyat

g ak

anna trit

tgt ak

anna tgit

af

af ak nn ka

g is

ikhf nk

Dfar nn

d uzrf ad nk

gh tudrt

yaZ nit gh ufuD wass nk

ad ak ur ajj

tazat n uswingm

ann tzziwz
afrak nk
ssugu grasn
aywa k
sgl ak
timDlt nk
ar d dik
ibDu iman
iddm as
i ughbalu
n matngh tifawt.

Made in the USA
Middletown, DE
15 June 2024

55835446R00035